USED AND FORGOTTEN
Book One

BY

Clarence W. Shook

Printed in the United States of America

Shook, Clarence W. 1931

ISBN: 1442168714

EAN 13:9781442168718

USED AND FORGOTTEN
Book One

BY
Clarence W. Shook

shookum@pldi.net

Table of Contents

PREFACE

While doing some research in 1980 on an early day photographer in South Central Oklahoma I fell in love with the area and bought a lot to build a lake cottage on.

In 1985 my wife and I decided to permanently move from Wichita Falls, Texas to Waurika Lake and built on to our lake cottage. During this time I sold my asphalt paving equipment but moved my earth moving equipment to the lake to do some work for the local farmers and the Corp of Engineer.

In the process I noticed all the old houses rich with weathered woods and remnants of the past that totally intrigued my photographic interest. They were a far cry from the hundreds and hundreds of photographs I had taken in color while I served my military obligation in France. These old stalwarts were void of the brilliance of my colored photography but had a pull and voice of their own. Part of that voice revisited my teen years when I had my own dark room and was deeply involved in learning black and white photography.

There were old deserted homestead remnants in South Central Oklahoma on nearly every quarter section of land. A few of the school buildings were yet standing but disappeared before I began my photographic essay of the past. Many of those first seen homesteads also have since met their demise as well.

After making visual recordings of the past in this area it just came natural to carry my camera everywhere we traveled throughout Oklahoma, Texas, Arkansas, New Mexico and Louisiana recording evidences of life as it used to be.

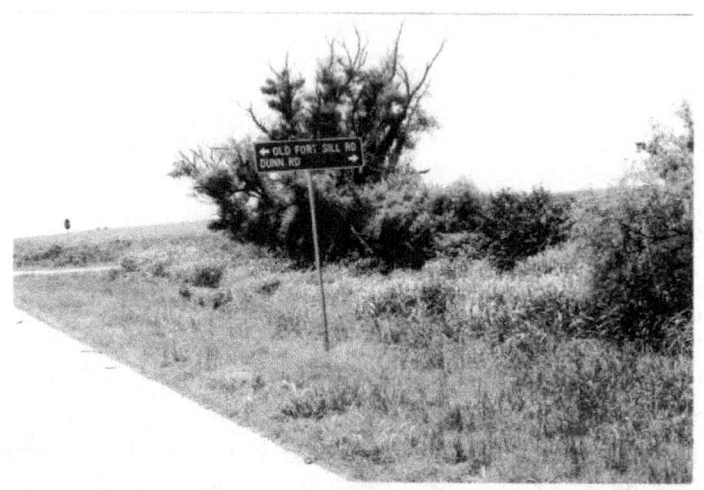

While my wife and I were searching the Old Fort Sill Road we found it just west of the Oklahoma/Texas Red River Bridge on Hwy. 79.

Chapter 1

Abandoned Homesteads in Jefferson, Cotton, and Stephens Counties in Oklahoma

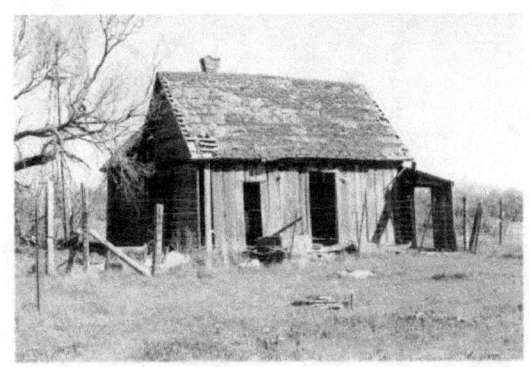

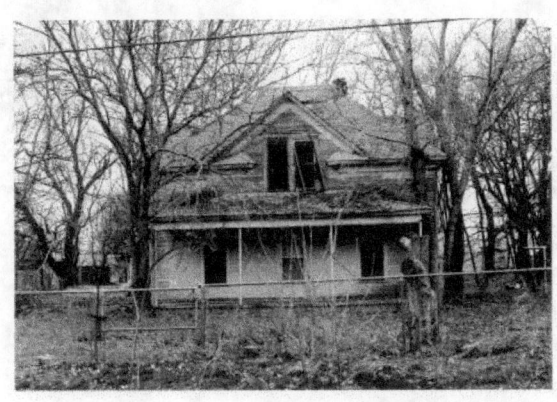

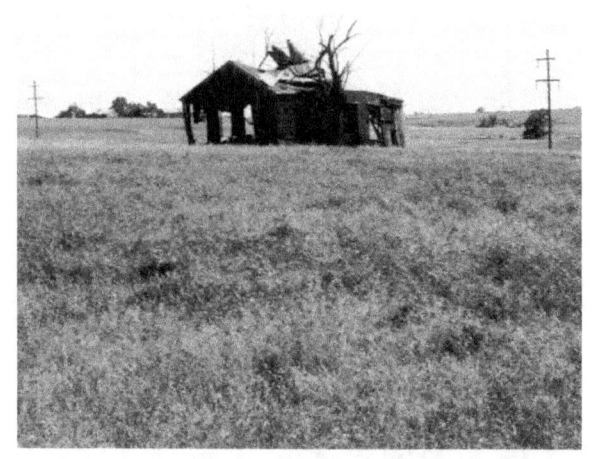

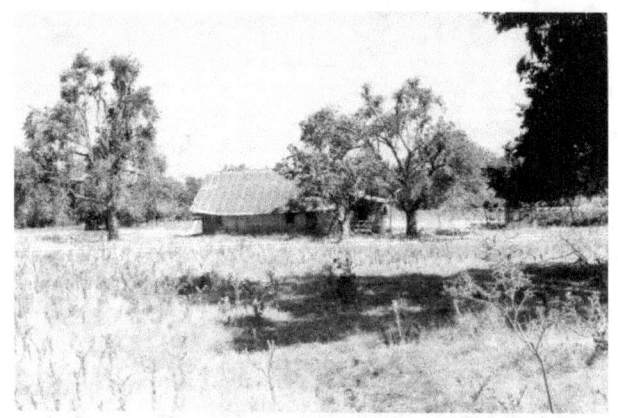

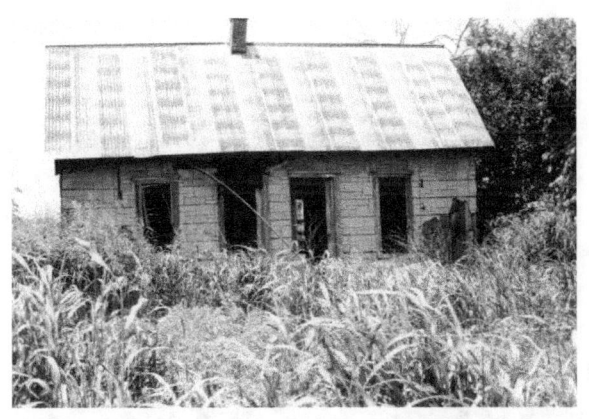

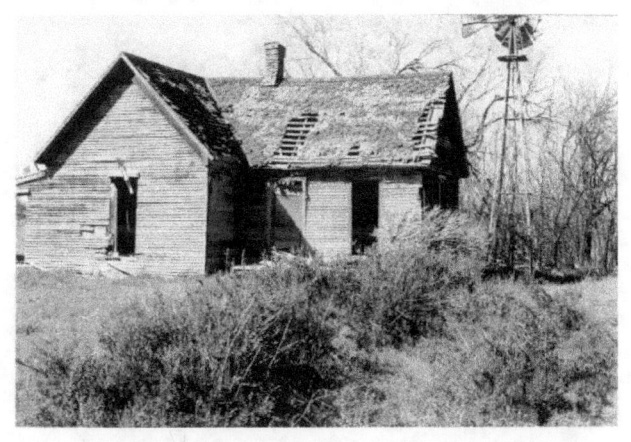

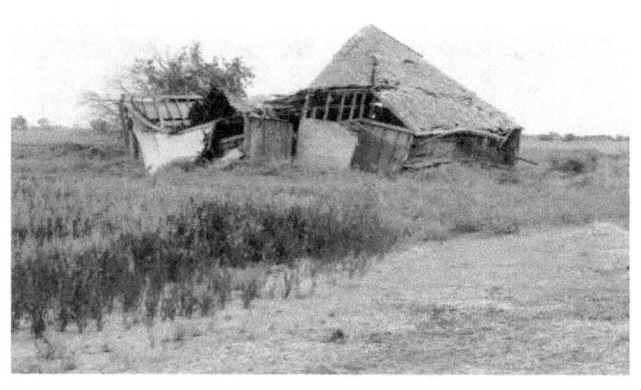

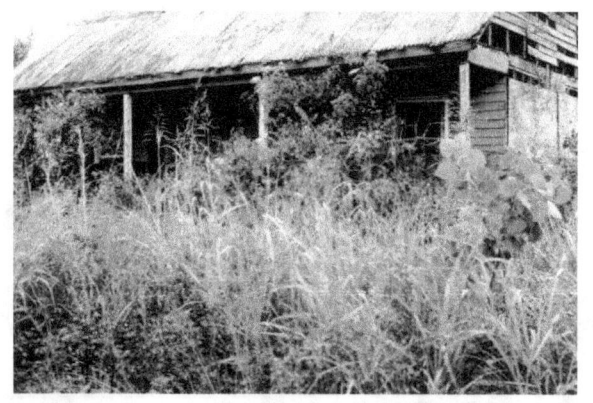

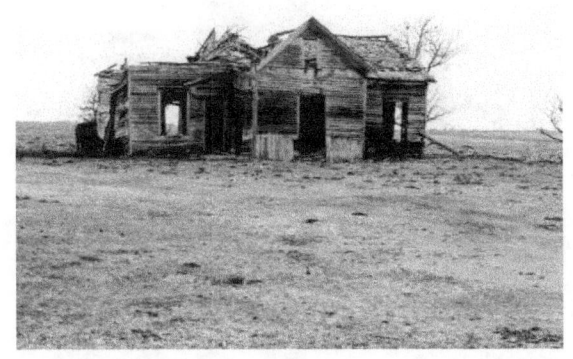

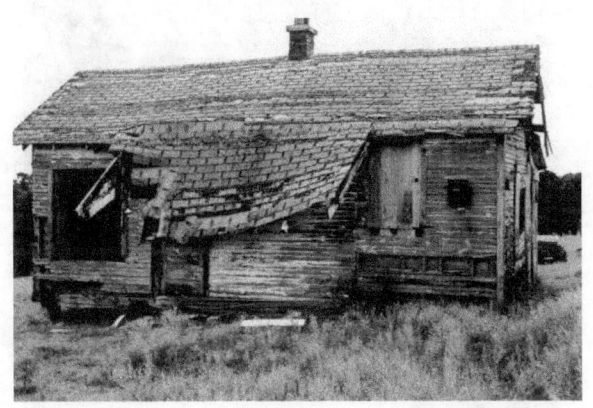

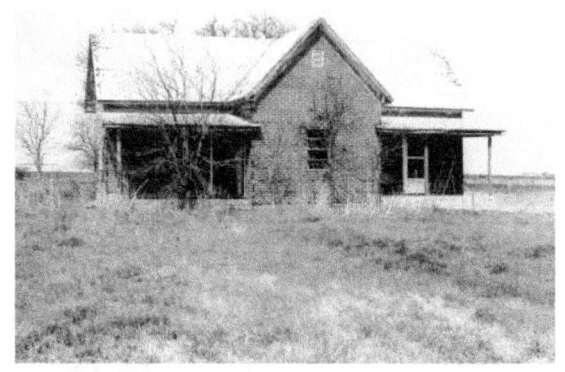

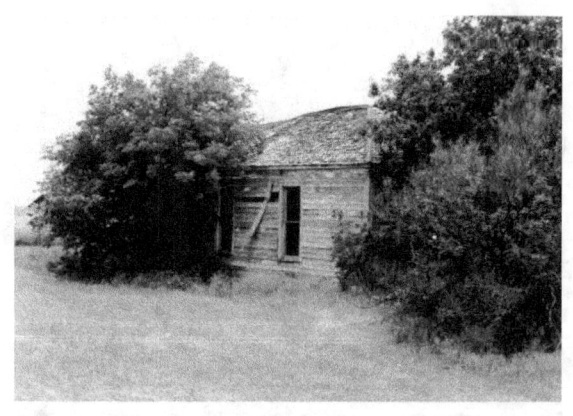

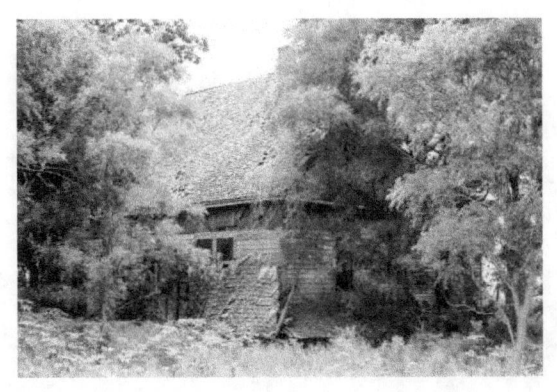

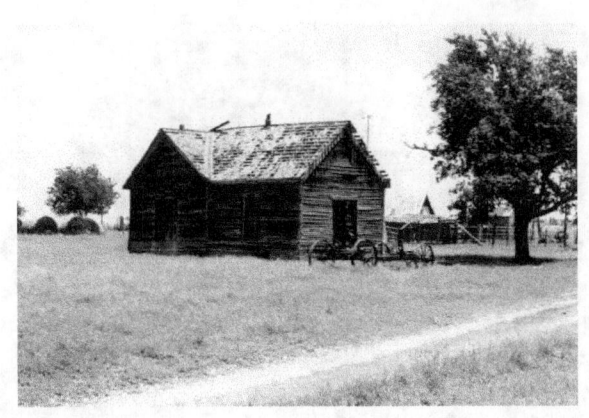

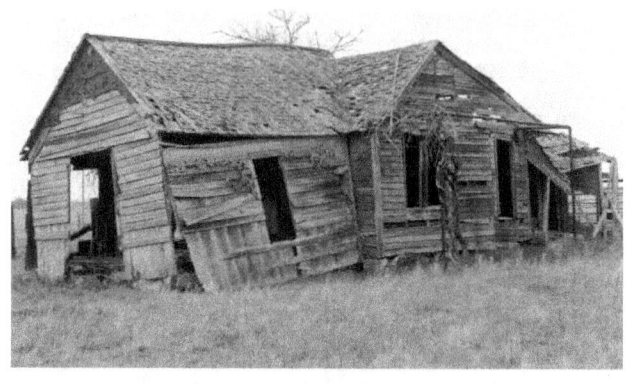

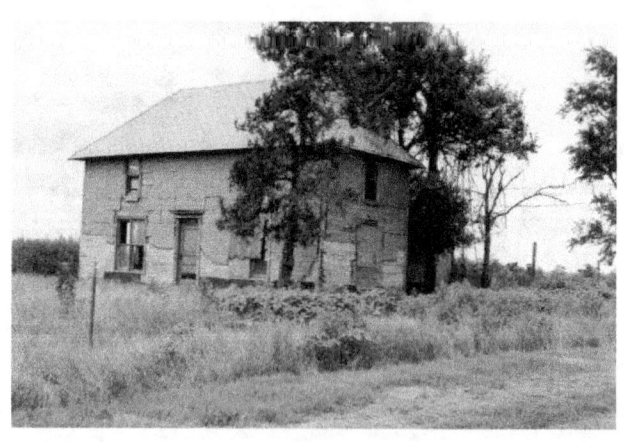

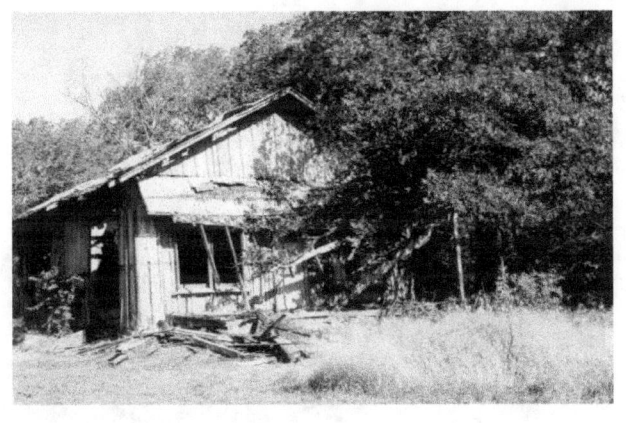

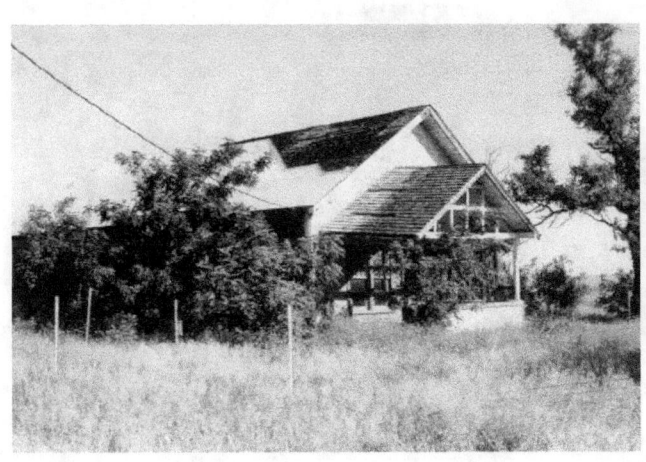

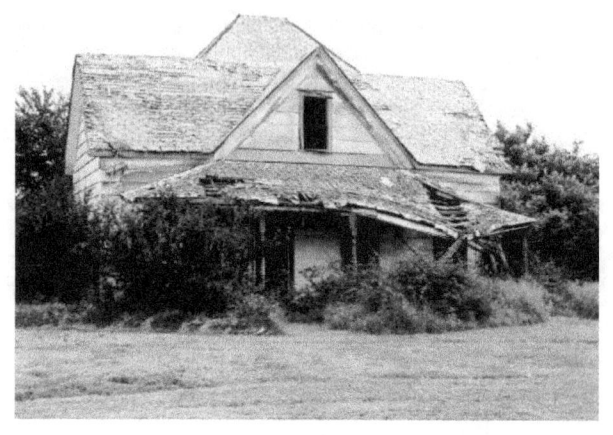

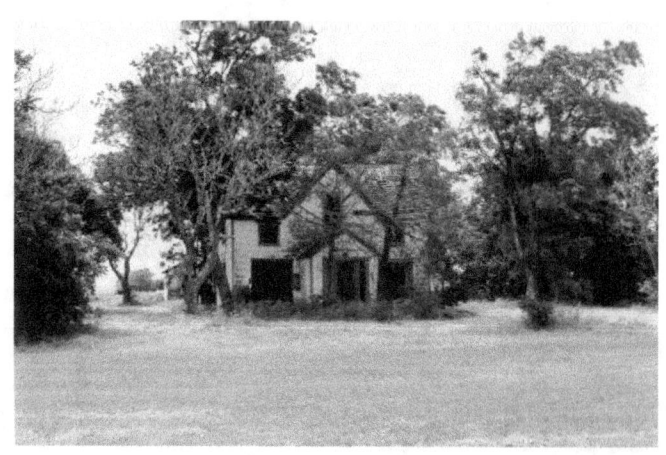

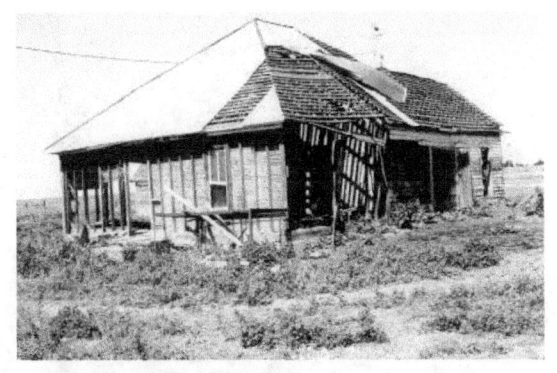

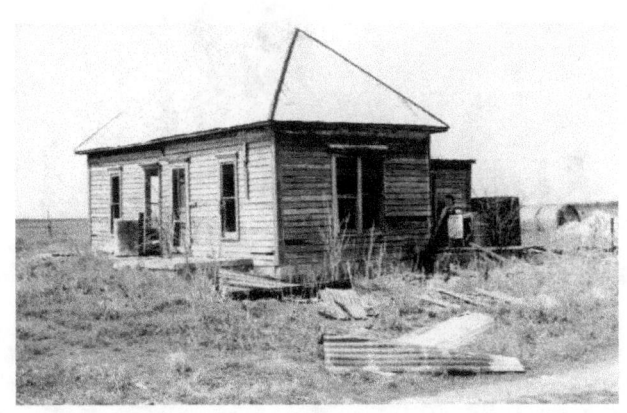

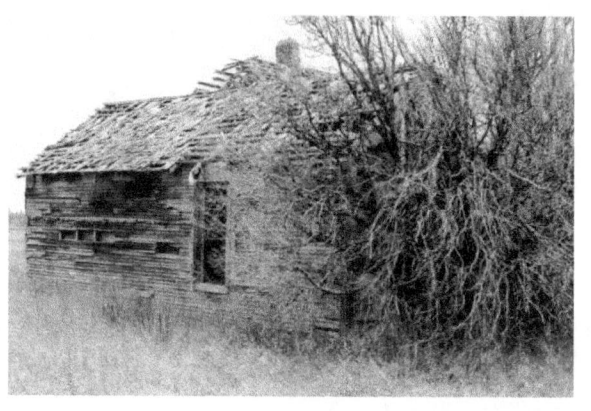

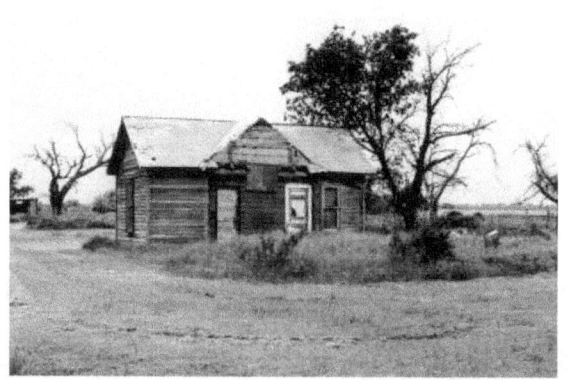

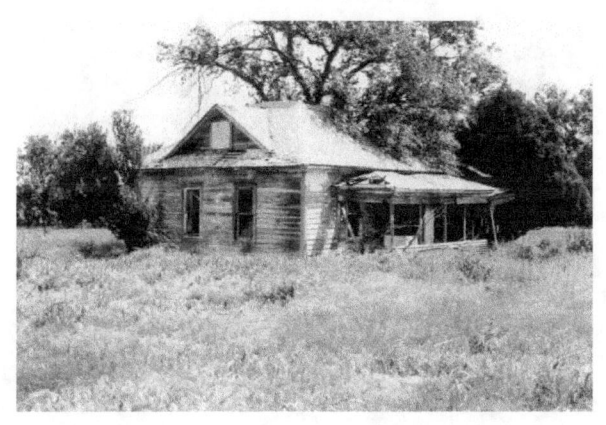

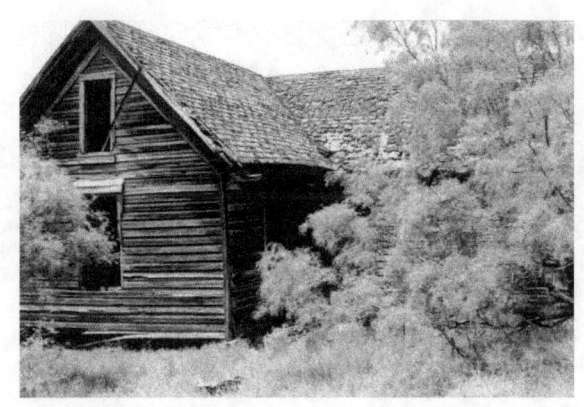

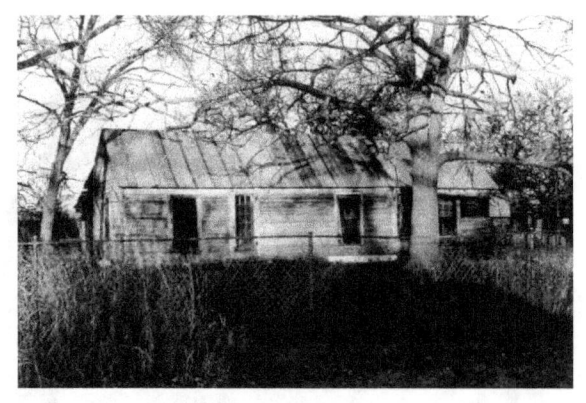

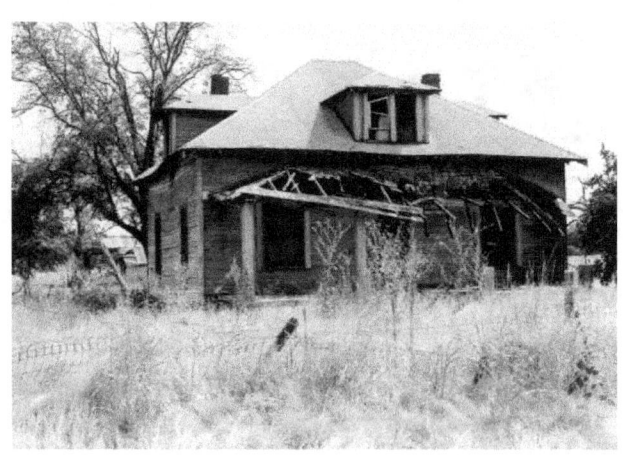

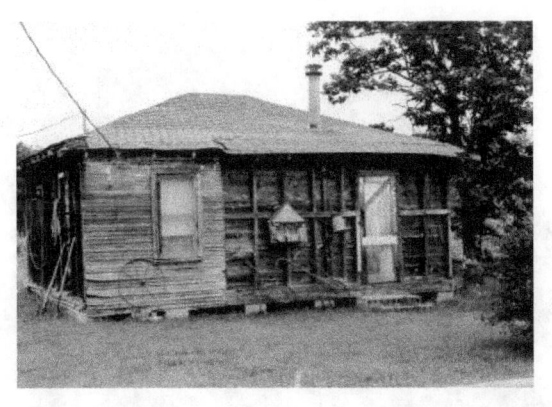

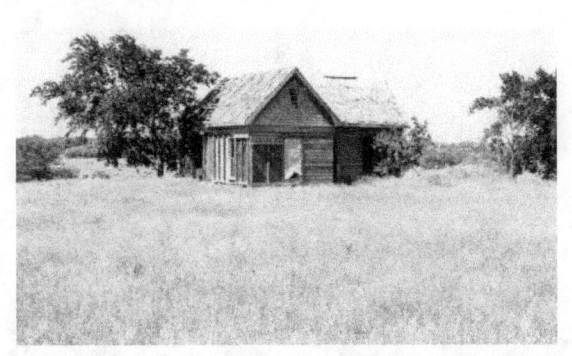

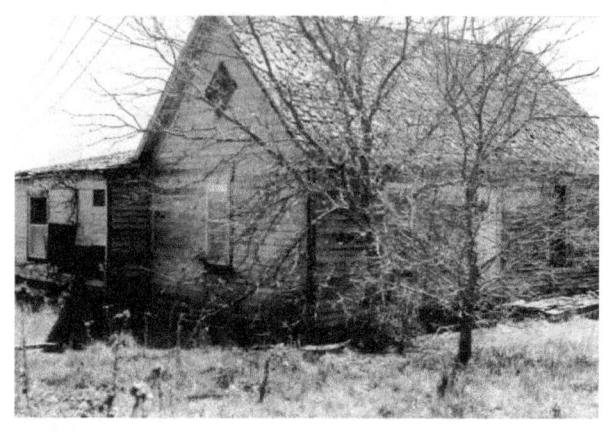

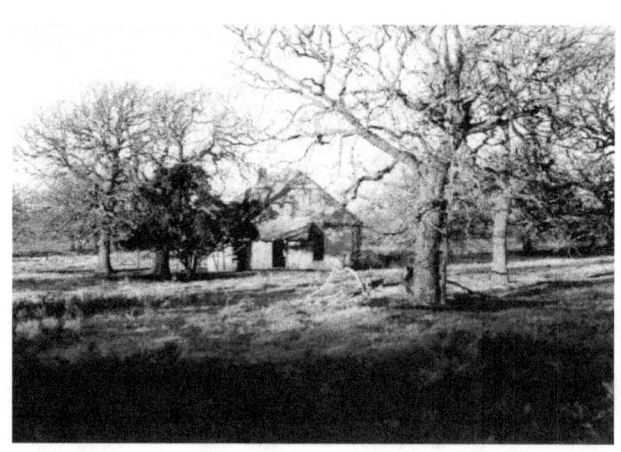

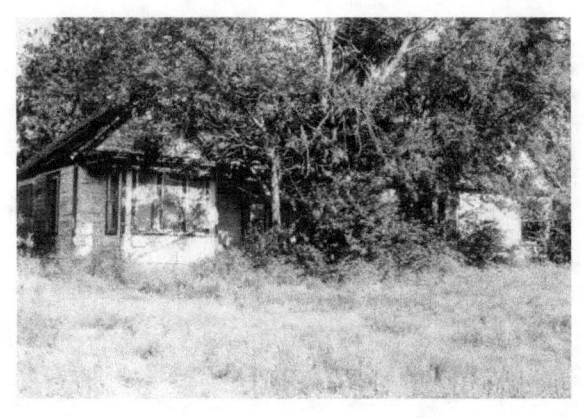

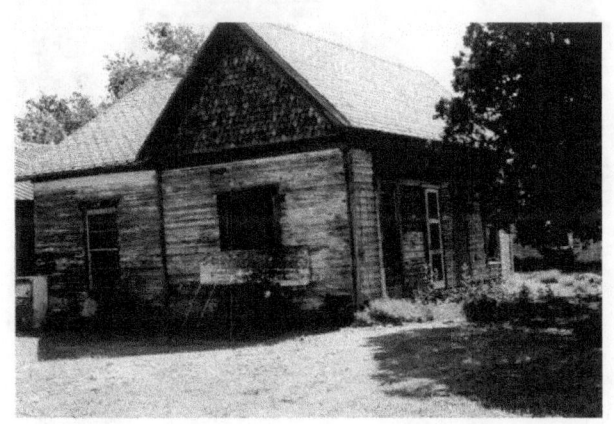

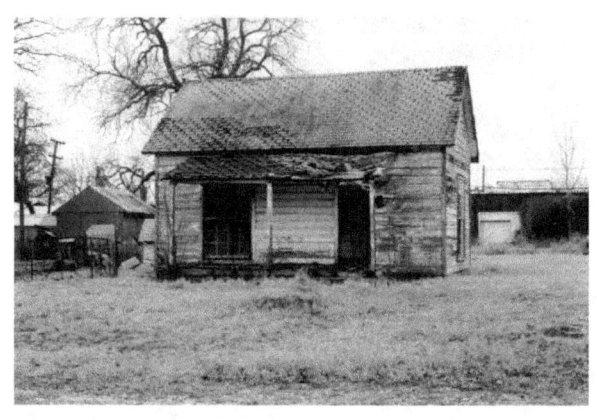

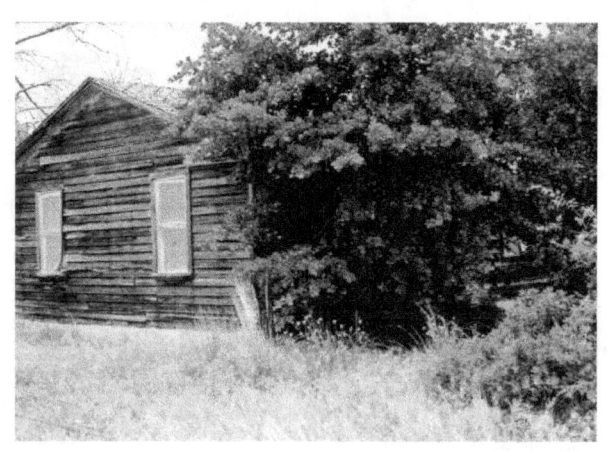

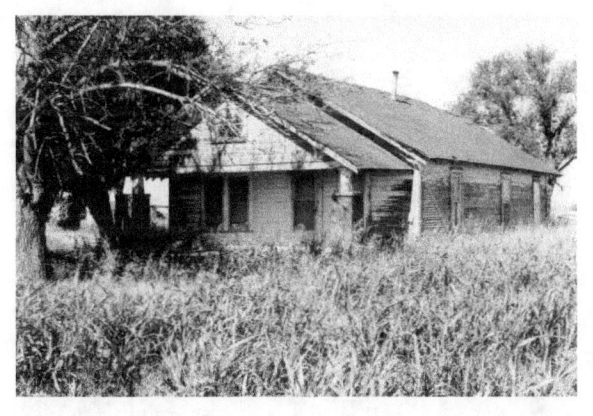

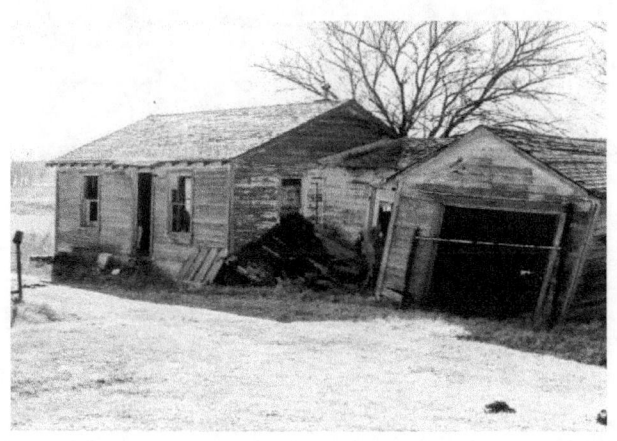

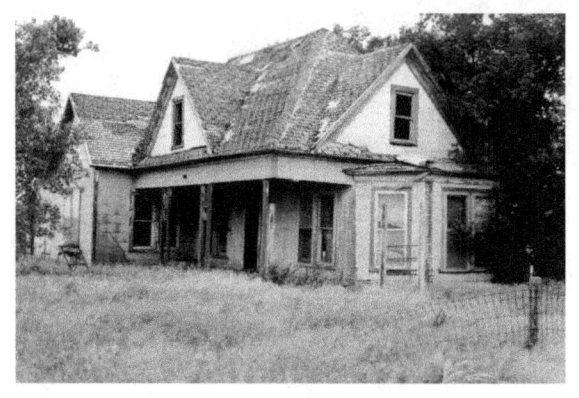

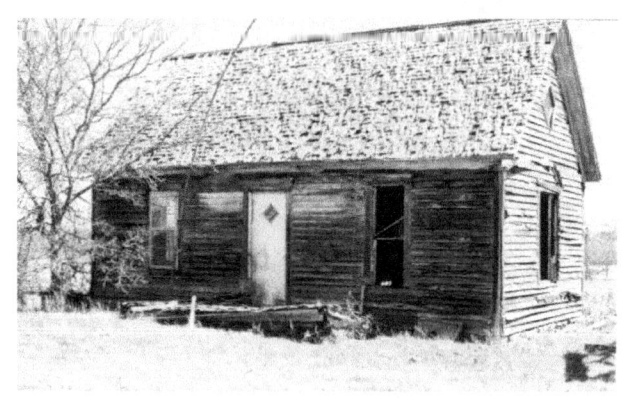

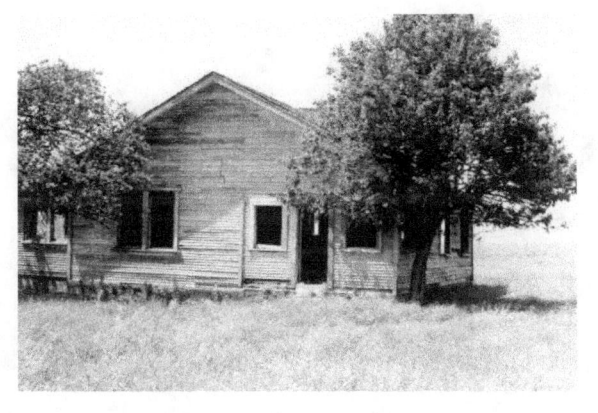

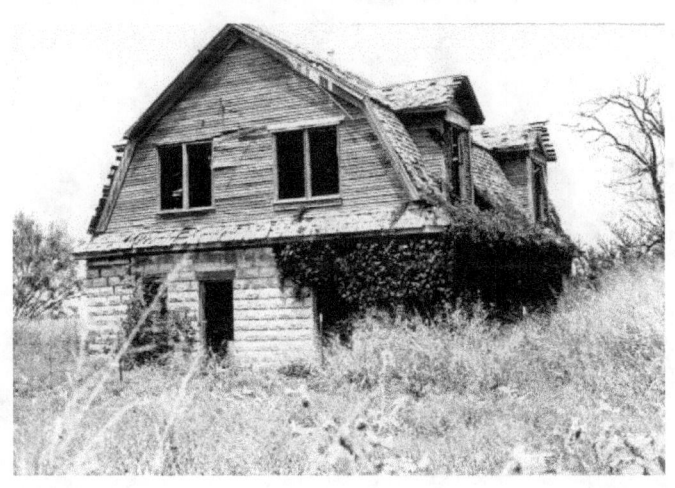

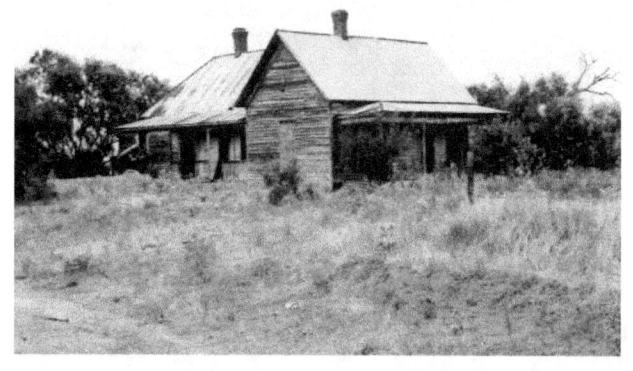

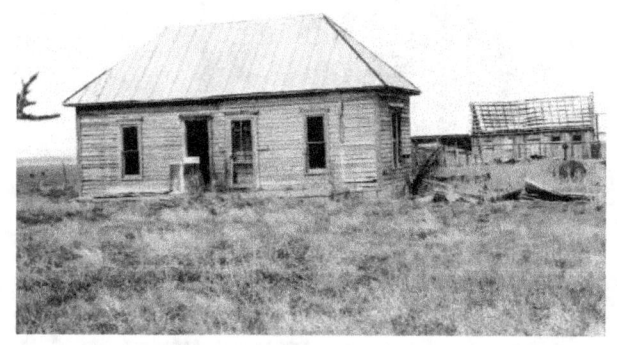

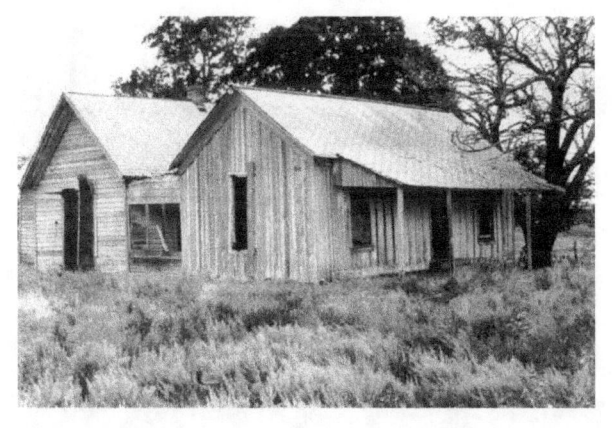

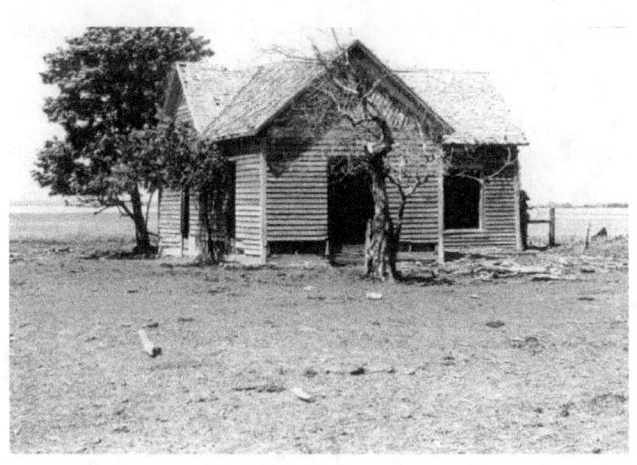

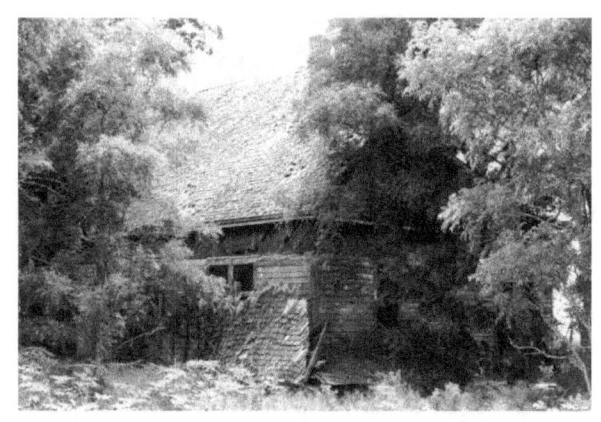

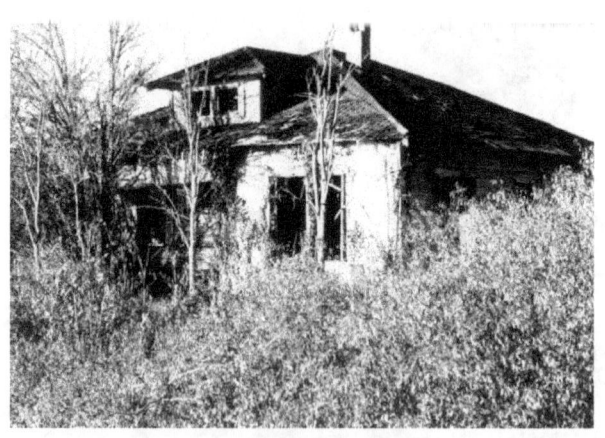

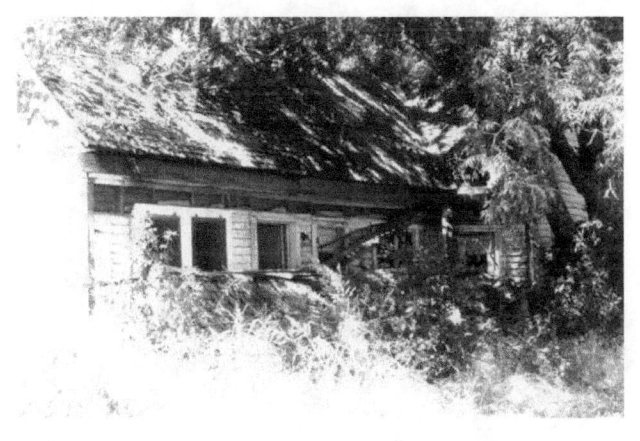

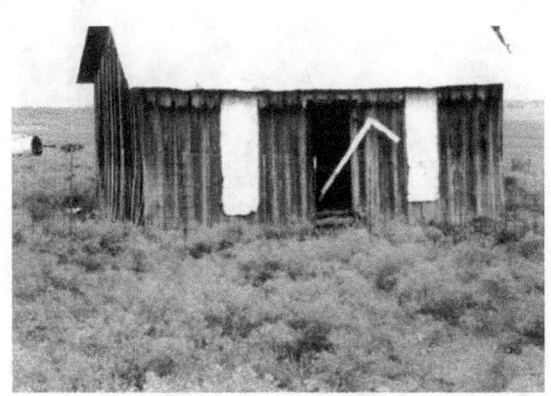

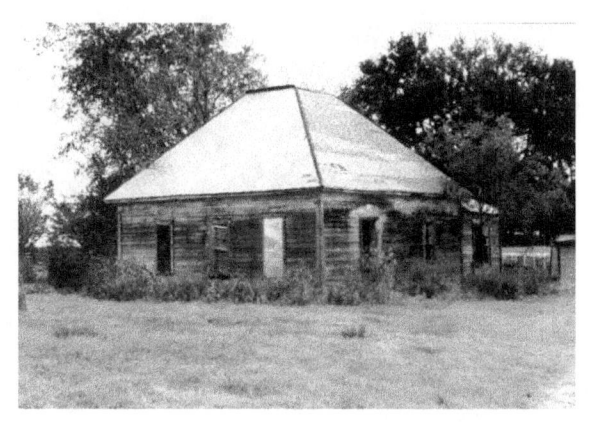

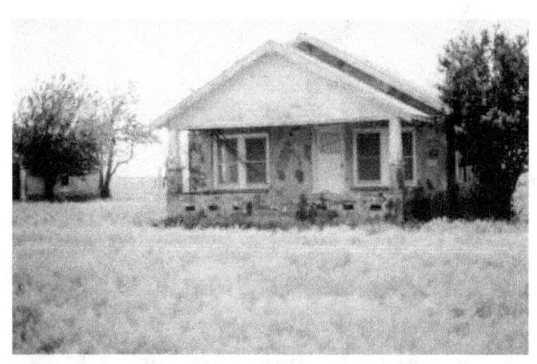

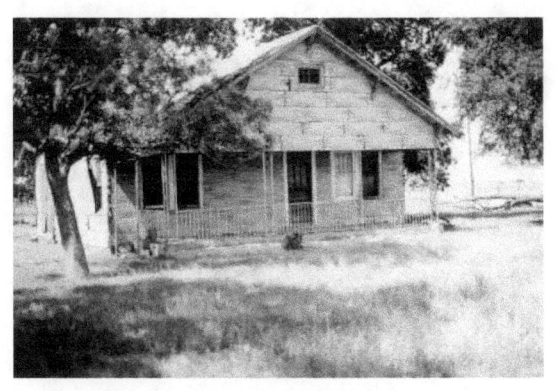

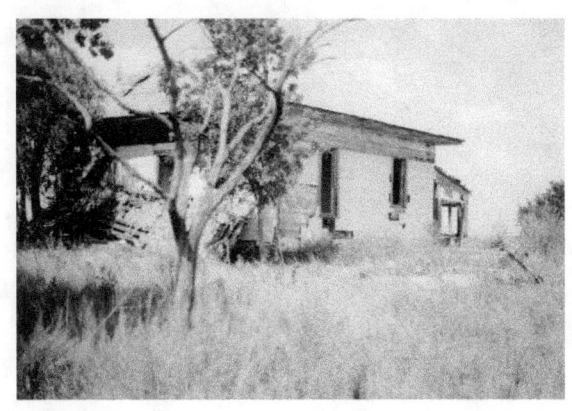

Chapter 2
Storm Cellar

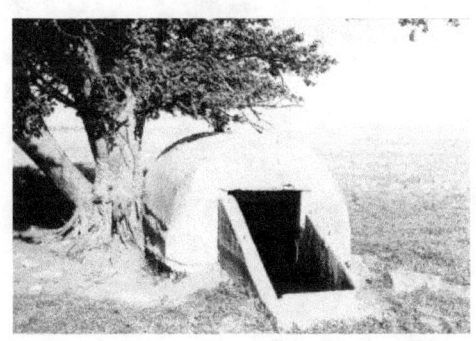

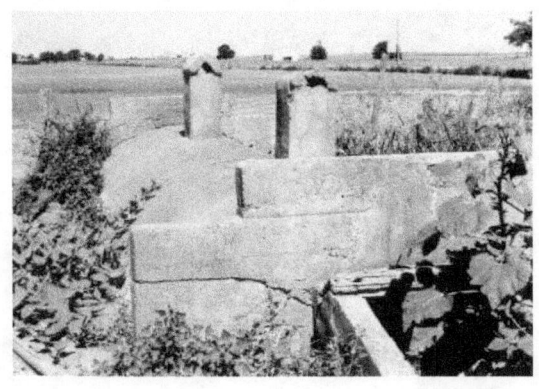

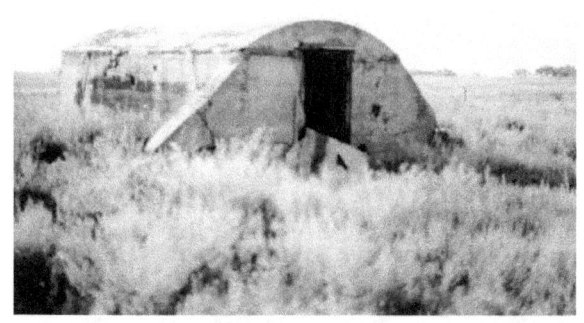

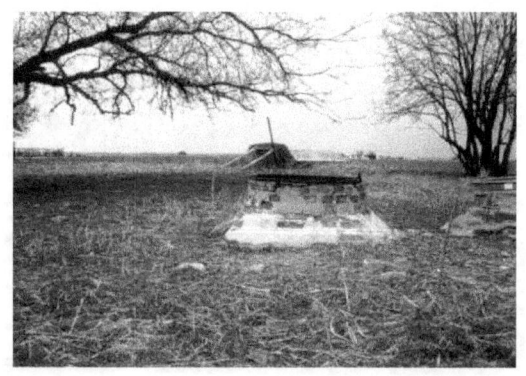

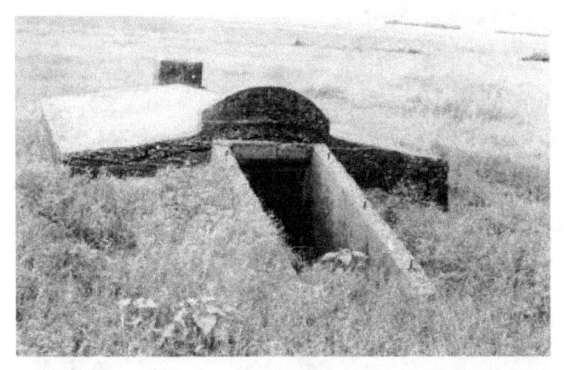

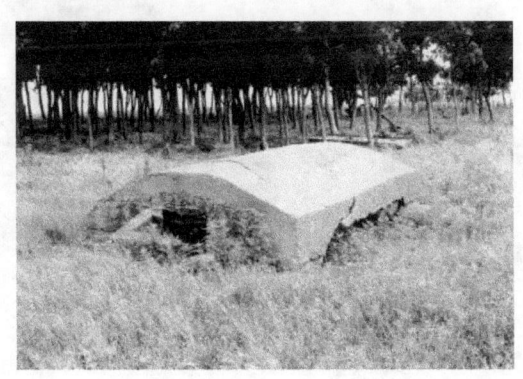

37

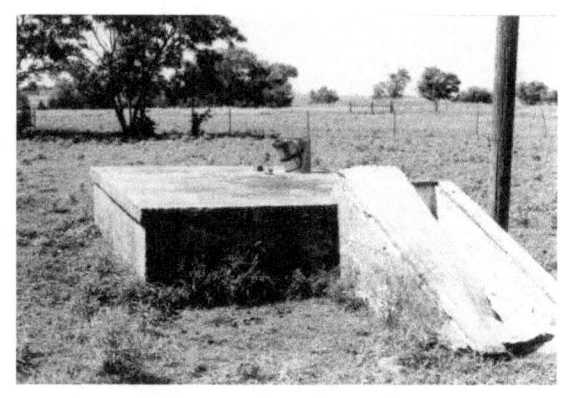

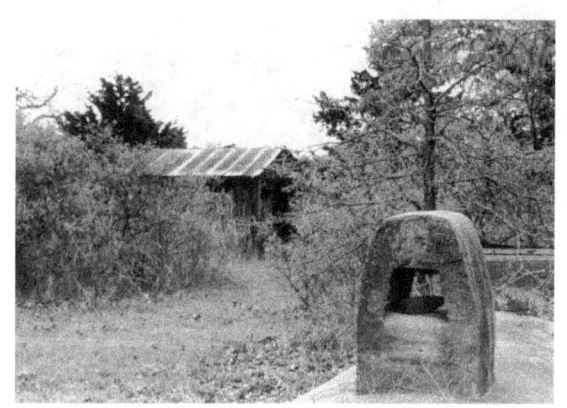

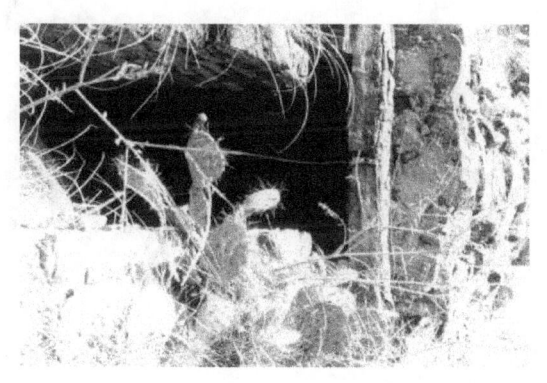

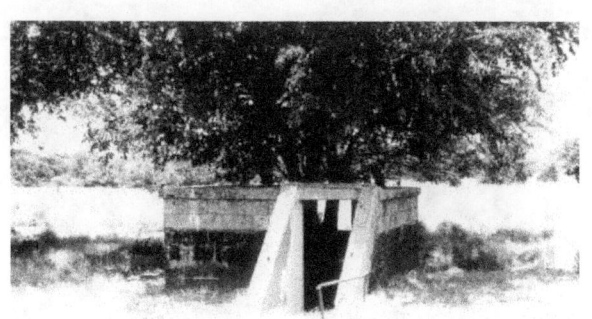

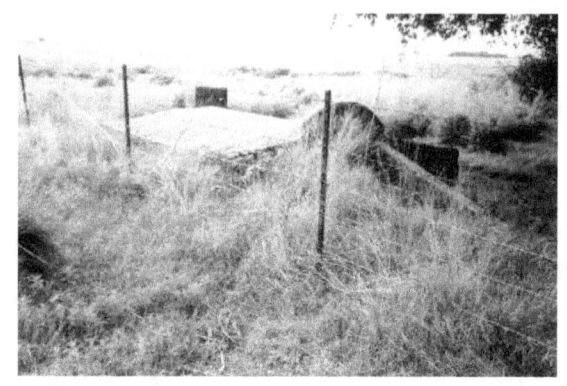

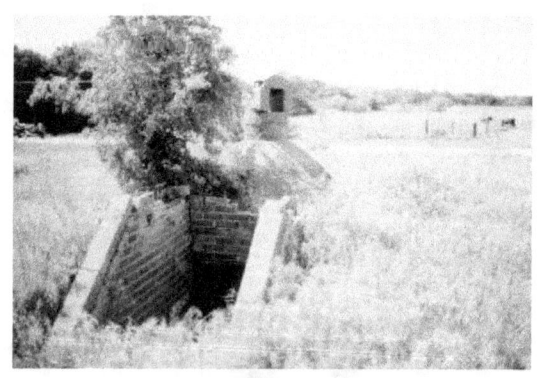

Chapter 3
Barnes

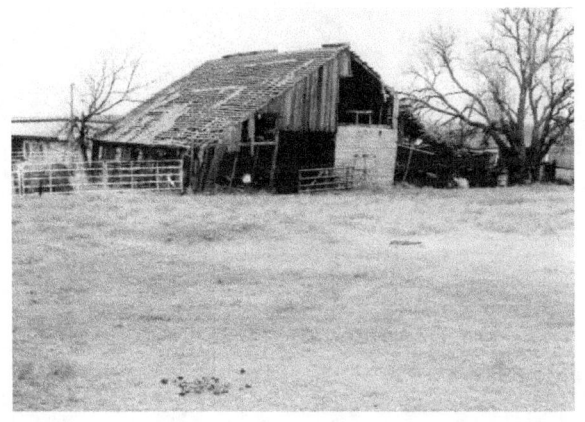

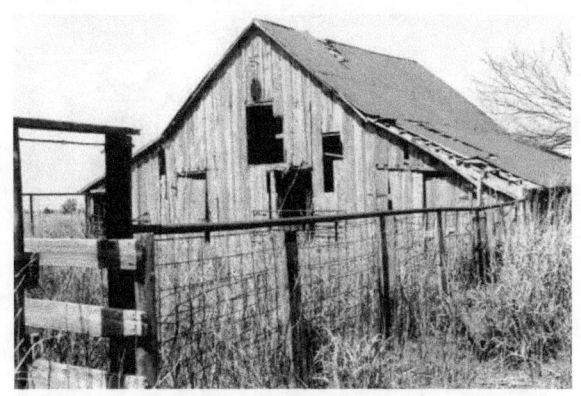

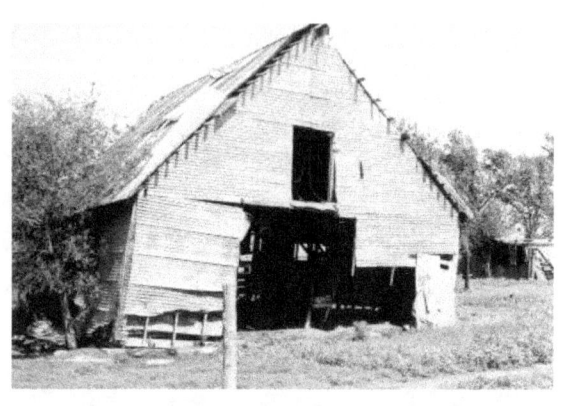

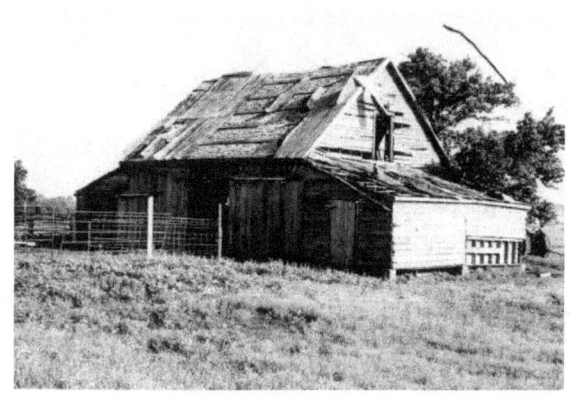

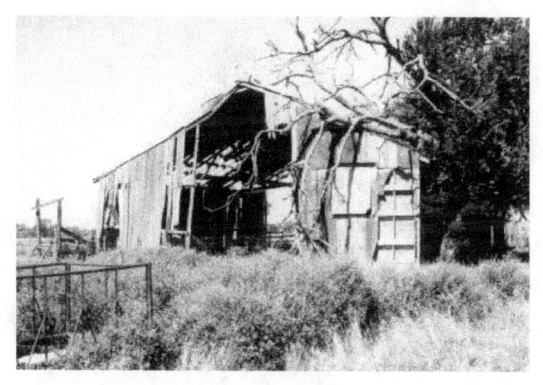

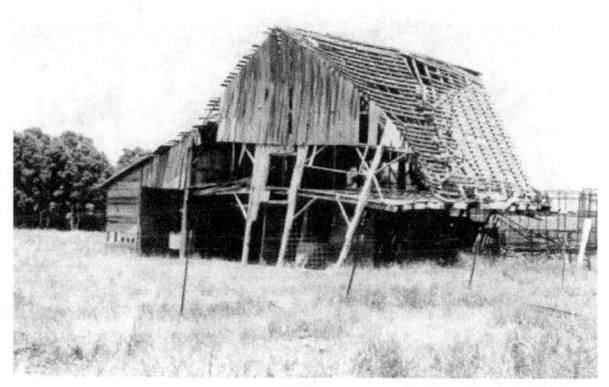

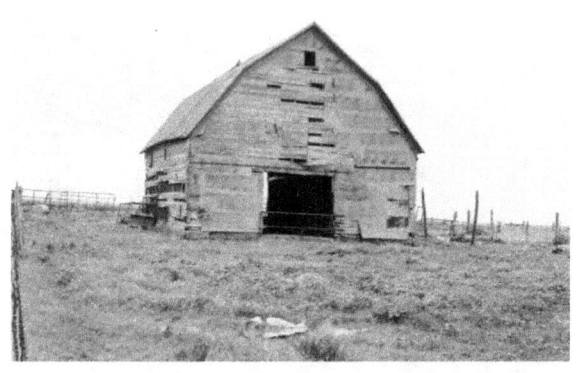

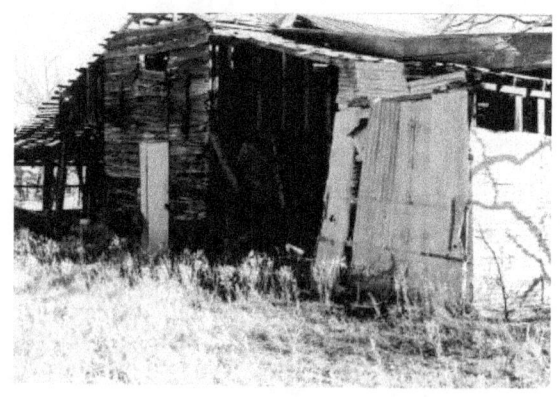

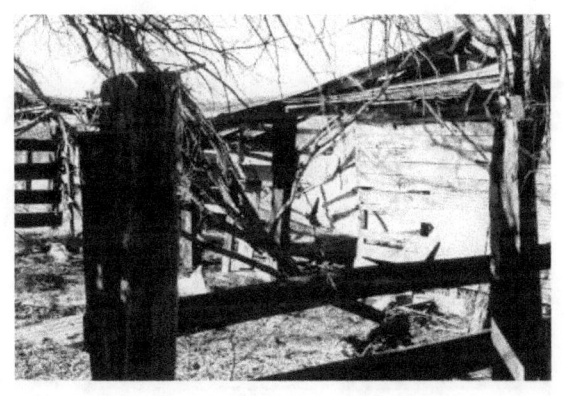

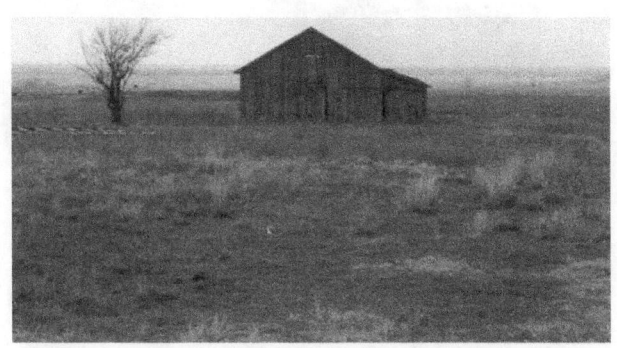

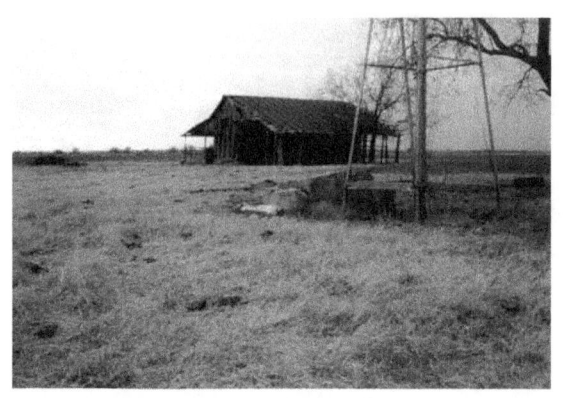

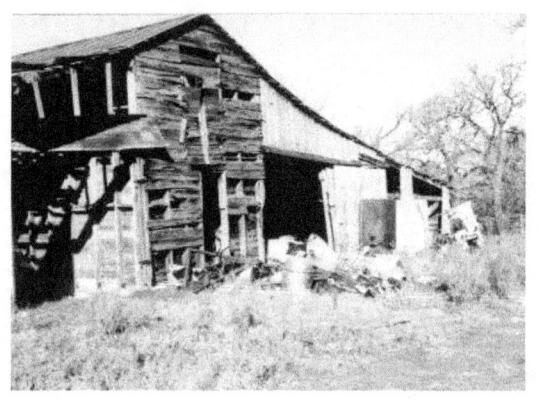

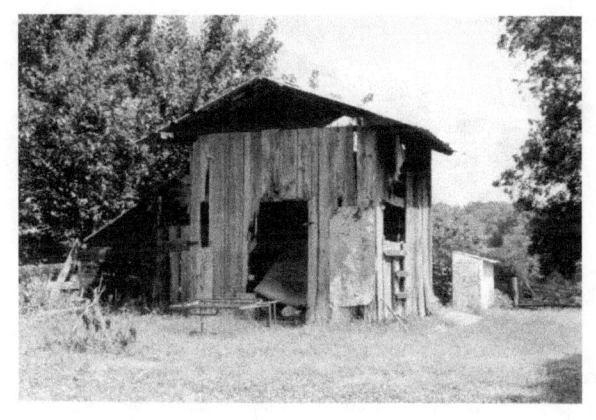

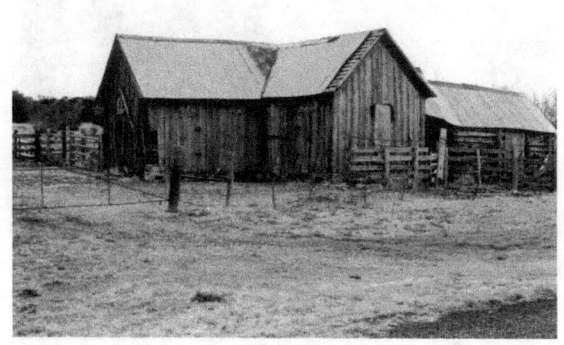

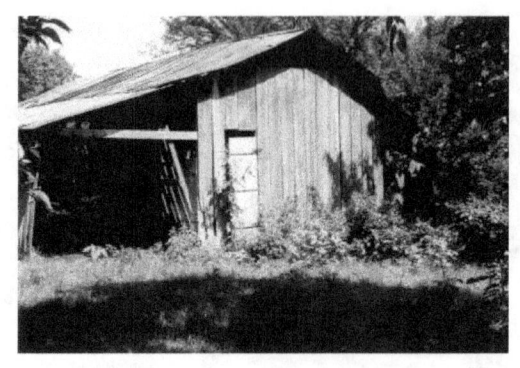

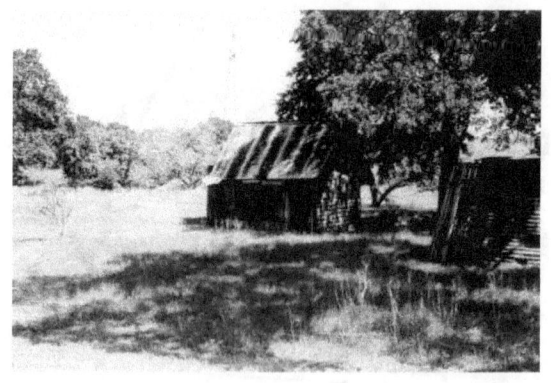

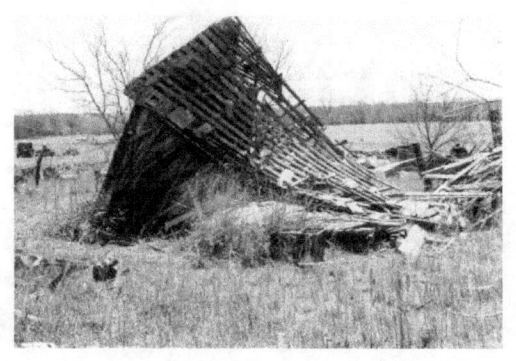

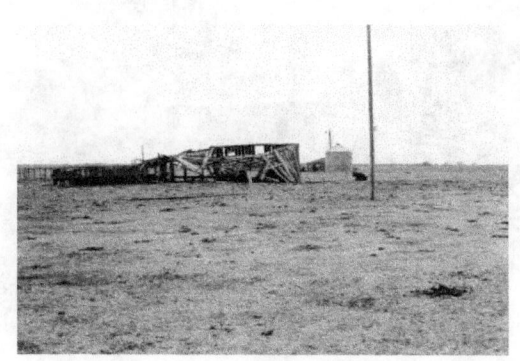

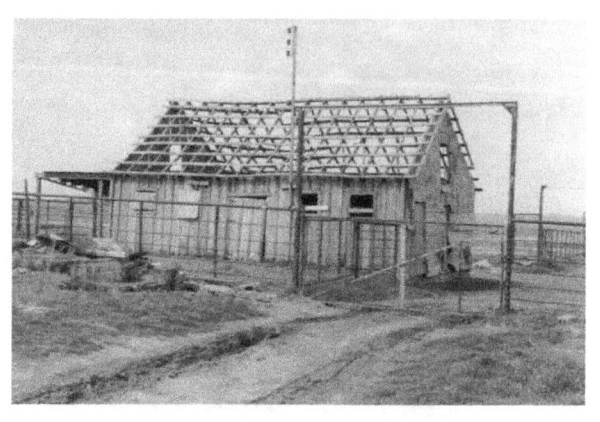

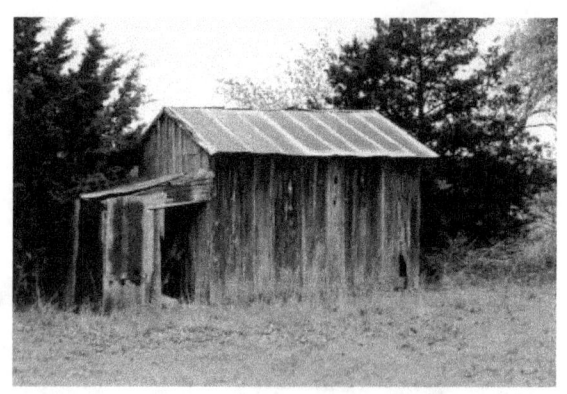

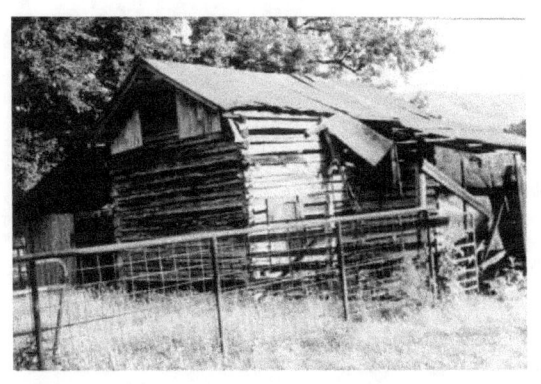

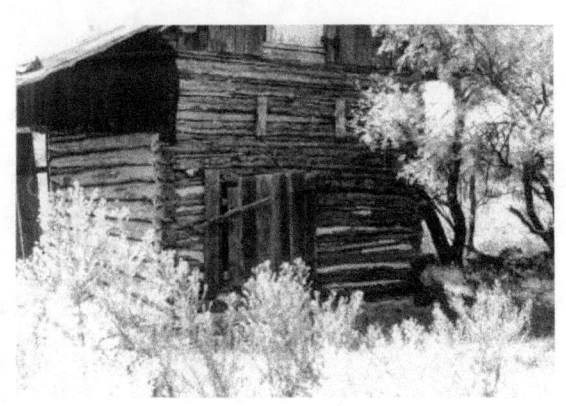

www.ingramcontent.com/pod-product-compliance
Lightning Source LLC
Chambersburg PA
CBHW051251170526
45165CB00004B/1667